HAND GANG JOKE BOOK

Francesca Simon spent her childhood on the beach in California, and then went to Yale and Oxford Universities to study medieval history and literature. She now lives in London with her family. She has written over fifty books and won the Children's Book of the Year in 2008 at the Galaxy British Book Awards for *Horrid Henry and the Abominable Snowman.*

Tony Ross is one of Britain's best known illustrators, with many picture books to his name as well as line drawings for many fiction titles. re.

Also by Francesca Simon
Don't Cook Cinderella
Helping Hercules

For younger readers
Café at the Edge of the Moon
Mr P's Naughty Book
The Parent Swap Shop
Illustrated by Pete Williamson

Spider School
Illustrated by Tony Ross

Barnyard Hullabaloo
Billy the Kid Goes Wild
Chicks Just Want to Have Fun
Mish Mash Hash
Moo Baa Baa Quack
Runaway Duckling
Where are my Lambs?
The Haunted House of Buffin Street
Jogger's Big Adventure
Look at Me
Meet the Gang
Miaow Miaow Bow Wow
Rampage in Prince's Garden
Yum Yum
The Topsy Turvies
Illustrated by Emily Bolam

There is a complete list of **Horrid Henry** titles at the end of the book.

Visit Horrid Henry's website at **www.horridhenry.co.uk** for competitions, games, downloads and a monthly newsletter!

HORRID HENRY'S PURPLE HAND GANG JOKE BOOK

Francesca Simon

Illustrated by Tony Ross

Orion
Children's Books

First published in Great Britain in 2011
by Orion Children's Books
a division of the Orion Publishing Group Ltd
Orion House
5 Upper Saint Martin's Lane
London WC2H 9EA
An Hachette UK Company

9 10 8

Jokes compiled by Sally Byford.

ISBN 978 1 4440 0163 1

A catalogue record for this book is available
from the British Library.

Printed in Great Britain by
Clays Ltd, St Ives plc

www.horridhenry.co.uk
www.orionbooks.co.uk

CONTENTS

Hello from Henry

Hey, everyone! I thought my other joke books had the horridest, wickedest, funniest and rudest jokes ever. But who knew my Purple Hand Gang would tell me so many GREAT jokes? Wow! Thanks for doing all the hard work, guys. I think I'll just stomp downstairs and drive Mum and Dad crazy with a few of these zingers. Way to go, gang. The Purple Hand Gang rules!

Henry

MY TOP PURPLE JOKES

What's purple and fixes pipes?
A plum-er.

Why did the elephant paint itself purple?
So it could hide in the plum tree.

Why are elephants big and grey?
If they were small and purple they'd be grapes.

What's purple and sounds like an ape?
A grape.

What's purple and barks at people?
A Grape Dane.

What happens when you drop
a purple rock in
the Red Sea?
It gets wet.

HENRY: There's a horrible big purple thing on your face!
DAD: Help! What is it?
HENRY: Your nose!

What's purple, brown and hairy?
Blackberry jam on toast stuck to the carpet.

What colour is a burp?
Burple

FAVOURITE JOKES FROM MY FANS

What do you get when you cross a cow and a werewolf?
A burger that bites back.

Did you hear about the fight outside the chippie last night?
Two fish got battered!

What did Mummy corn say to Baby corn?
Where's Pop corn?

Waiter, Waiter, why is there a footprint on my cake?
Because you said step on it.

Why didn't the elephant board his plane?
Because it wasn't a jumbo.

Which ghost stops goals?
A ghoulkeeper.

Which are the three most famous poles?
North, South and Tad.

What do you call a daft dinosaur?
Idiotsaurus.

Why are bananas so good at gymnastics?
They are great at doing the splits.

What's a polygon?
A dead parrot.

Where did the spaghetti dance?
At the meatball.

What do you call
a lion without
any eyes?
Lon.

Doctor, Doctor, I
only have 50
seconds to live.
Just give me a minute.

Knock knock.
Who's there?
Justin.
Justin who?
Justin in time to let me in, toad.

What do you get when you cross a cat and a parrot?
A carrot.

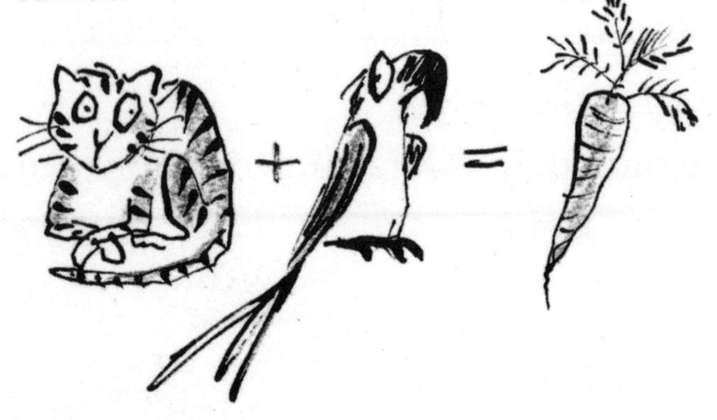

Who is a penguin's favourite aunt?
Aunt Arctica.

Why did the boy put sugar on his pillow?
He wanted to have sweet dreams.

What do you call a donkey with one eye and three legs?
A winky wonky donkey.

Why are insects clever?
Because they always know when you're having a picnic.

What do you get when you cross a bomb and a bad smell?
A stinkbomb.

Doctor, Doctor, I can't sleep at night.
Lie on the edge of your bed and you'll soon drop off.

What goes black white black white black white?
A penguin rolling down a hill.

What goes black white black white black white, HA HA?
The penguin that pushed him.

Why did the mushroom enjoy the party so much?
Because he's a fungi.

What was the magical secret agent called?
James Wand.

Did I tell you the joke about butter?
I'd better not in case you spread it.

Waiter, Waiter, will my pizza be long?
No, sir, it'll be round.

Why are adults always complaining?
Because they are groan ups.

Who did Frankenstein
take to the party?
His ghoulfriend.

What do you call a scared octopus?
An octopussy.

How does a cowboy ride into town on
Friday, stay for three days and ride
out on Friday?
His horse is called Friday!

What's an astronaut's favourite place on the keyboard?
The spacebar.

What do hedgehogs like to eat?
Prickled onions.

What do mother penguins tell their children when they go out?
Beak careful.

Why does a cow have a bell?
Because its horns don't work.

Why did the cow cross the road?
To get to the udder side.

Why did the cow cross the road again?
It wanted to see a moooooovie.

What do you call a scared biscuit?
A cowardy custard cream.

What do you get when you cross a sheep with a kangaroo?
A woolly jumper.

Knock knock.
Who's there?
Cash.
Cash who?
No thanks, I prefer peanuts.

Why did the biscuit go to the doctors?
Because he felt crummy.

What's the difference between roast beef and pea soup?
Anyone can roast beef but nobody can pea soup.

Why don't leopards cheat in exams?
They know they'll be spotted.

What do you call a man with a seagull on his head?
Cliff.

Waiter, Waiter, there's a small slug in my salad.
Sorry, Madam, would you like a bigger one?

What do you call a woodpecker with no beak?
A headbanger.

MISS BATTLE-AXE: Today I want you to write an essay on a goldfish.
RUDE RALPH: I can't do that.
MISS BATTLE-AXE: Why not?
RUDE RALPH: Because I don't have any waterproof ink.

Why is Europe like a frying pan?
It has Greece at the bottom.

Doctor, Doctor, I feel like a cow.
Sit there and don't moooooove.

What is a ghost's favourite food?
Spookhetti.

The three bears came home. Daddy Bear said, "Who's been eating my porridge?" and Mummy Bear said, "Who's been eating my porridge?" and Baby Bear said, "Never mind about the porridge, who's nicked the telly!"

What do you call
a computer superhero?
A screen saver.

How do you get a baby astronaut to sleep?
Rocket.

Why couldn't the orange run up the hill?
It ran out of juice.

Why can't a monster's head be
12 inches long?
Because then it would be a foot.

Where do wasps go when they're hurt?
To the waspital.

What do you call a sleeping bull?
A bulldozer.

A butcher is two metres tall and wears size thirteen shoes. What does he weigh?
Meat.

What do you get when you cross Dr Frankenstein with a pig?
Frankenswine.

What do computers eat?
Microchips.

What do you call a lion with toothache?
Rory.

What does an octopus wear when it's cold?
A coat of arms.

Where do you catch a flying pig?
At the airpork.

What do you call a fish with no eye?
A fsh.

MISS BATTLE-AXE: Name the four seasons.
GREEDY GRAHAM: Salt, pepper, mustard and vinegar.

What's the cleverest species of dinosaur?
A Thesaurus.

Who shouted knickers at the big bad wolf?
Little rude riding hood.

Why did the boy carry a clock
and a bird on Halloween?
For tick or tweet.

Knock knock.
Who's there?
Bacon.
Bacon who?
Bacon a cake for your birthday.

What do you get when you cross a computer with an elephant?
Lots of memory.

What did the frog order at the fast food restaurant?
French flies and a diet croak.

What goes up the stairs but never moves?
A carpet.

How do you make a fruit punch?
Give it boxing lessons.

What do you call a man with a map on his head?
Miles.

Who gives presents to children, then gobbles them up?
Santa Jaws.

How do snails keep their shells so shiny?
They use snail varnish.

What do witches put on their hair?
Scare spray.

Which painting is never happy?
The Moaning Lisa.

What are the werewolves' cousins called?
The whywolf, the whatwolf and the whenwolf.

Can I tell you a joke about a wall?
Yes please.
No, because you'll never get over it.

A man came round to our house asking for donations for the local swimming pool. I gave him a glass of water!

What does a ghost call his mum and dad?
Transparents.

What's the Earth's favourite bit of a pizza?
The crust.

What do cows eat for breakfast?
MOOOuesli.

Which two letters are bad for your teeth?
DK.

What does a dentist do on a rollercoaster?
He braces himself.

What did the elf use to make himself taller?
Elf raising flour.

Why was the skeleton afraid of the dog?
Because dogs like bones!

What do you get when you cross
a pig and a woodchopper?
Pork chops.

What do you call James Bond in the bath?
Bubble O Seven.

What do you call a woman with two toilets on her head?
Lulu.

DAD: I hope you're not talking in class any more.
HORRID HENRY: I'm not talking any more, I'm talking the same amount.

I saw Esau sitting on a see-saw.
How many s's in that?
There aren't any s's in THAT!

Doctor, Doctor, I've got a strawberry growing on my head.
Well, put some cream on it.

What runs but has no legs?
Water.

Waiter, Waiter, do you serve fish?
Sit down, Sir, we serve anyone.

What did the plumber say to his wife when their marriage ended?
It's over flow.

What's the sweetest insect?
A humbug.

Knock knock.
Who's there?
Egbert.
Egbert who?
Egbert no bacon.

What do you call a rooster that wakes you up at the same time every morning?
An alarm cluck.

What do you call a skeleton snake?
A rattler.

What's the difference between an African elephant and an Indian elephant?
About 6,000 kilometres.

MUM: Shall I put the kettle on?
DAD: No, I prefer the dress you're wearing now.

LADY: Can I try that dress on in the window?
SHOPKEEPER: No way, try it on in the changing room.

Doctor, Doctor, I think I'm shrinking.
Well, you'll have to be a little patient.

What happened to the cat that
ate a ball of wool?
She had mittens.

What has 22 legs, 11 heads and 2 wings?
A football team.

A bee just stung me on my arm.
Which one?
I don't know, they all look the same to me.

Why did the sheep cross the road?
It wanted to go to the baaaarbers.

What do you call a bee that lives in a graveyard?
A zom-bee.

What cheese is made backwards?
Edam.

Doctor, Doctor, I keep thinking I'm a canary.
Perch yourself down and I'll tweet you in a minute.

What did the ghost teacher say to her pupils?
Look at the board – I'm going to go through it again.

What do you get when you dial 34027358923759235872935873359857?
A sore finger.

Why do hens watch TV?
For hentertainment.

Why is my brother built upside down?
Because his nose runs and his feet smell.

What did one volcano say to the other volcano?
Do you lava me like I lava you?

What do you get when you cross a cow, a sheep and a baby goat?
The Milky Baa kid.

Why did the submarine go red?
Because it saw the ship's bottom.

What did the parrot take for his headache?
Parrotcetemol.

A horse went up to two cows and said, "Excuse me, where are the toilets?"
"That's amazing," said one cow to the other, "a horse that can speak."

What do you call a man with a tree growing out of his head?
Edward.

Why did a man with one hand cross the road?
To get to the second hand shop.

One day a man was walking down the street with a penguin. A policeman saw them and told the man to take the penguin to the zoo. The next day the policeman saw the man again with the penguin, and said, "I thought I told you to take the penguin to the zoo." The man said, "I did, and we had such fun that I'm taking him to the cinema today."

What's black when you buy it, red when you use it and grey when you throw it away?
Coal.

What's a sheep's favourite snack?
Chocolate baaaaaars.

There were three cookies in the jar last night and now there's only one. What's your excuse?
It was dark so I must have missed it!

What do you call a man who likes fishing?
Rod.

What did the chick say when his mum laid an orange?
Look what marmalade.

What does an alien from Mars like to eat?
Martian-mallows.

Why do zebras like old movies?
Because they are black and white.

What happened to the wooden car with the wooden wheels and the wooden engine?
It wooden go.

What did the teacher say when the horse walked into the classroom?
Why the long face?

What are a monster's favourite fairground rides?
The helter skeleton and the roller ghoster.

How does a dog stop the DVD player?
He presses the paws button.

A guest in a posh hotel says to the waiter, "Can I order two boiled eggs, one undercooked and runny and one overcooked and tough, with some rubbery bacon and burnt toast."

The waiter said, "Sir, we can't serve such a dreadful breakfast!"

"Why not?" the guest replied. "That's what I got here yesterday!"

Knock knock.
Who's there?
A dare.
A dare who?
A dare once, but I'm bald now.

Why do dogs run round in circles?
It's hard to run in squares.

What do you call a skunk that's disappeared?
Ex-stinked.

What has a bed but never sleeps?
A river.

Why did the bald man stick his head out of the window?
To get some fresh hair.

Which travels faster – heat or cold?
Heat, because you can catch a cold.

How do you make a jacket last?
Make the trousers first.

Why is history like a fruitcake?
It's full of dates.

What did the scarf say to the hat?
You go on ahead and I'll hang around.

What comes once in a minute, twice in a moment, but never in a thousand years?
The letter M.

What smells worse than a skunk?
Two skunks.

Did you hear about the wolves' all-night party?
It was a howling success.

When do birds celebrate their dads?
On feather's day.

What do you call an animal that talks too much?
A yak.

Why did Santa have to close his factory?
For elf and safety.

What do you get when you cross a cow and an earthquake?
A milkshake.

Why don't oysters share?
Because they're shellfish.

What do you call a parrot with no wings?
A walkie talkie.

How do you catch a rabbit?
Hide behind a tree and
make a noise like a carrot.

What can you serve but can't eat?
Tennis balls.

What did the lion say when he saw two men in a car?
Yum, yum, meals on wheels.

Why did the robber take a bath?
He wanted to make a clean getaway.

Why did the overweight man throw his wallet in the bin?
He wanted to lose a couple of pounds.

Which vehicle is the same going backwards or forwards?
Racecar.

What's the best place for a mouse to leave its boat?
The hickory dickory dock.

Why was the broom late for breakfast?
It overswept.

How can you swallow a plug?
Gulp backwards.

What goes 'oom oom'?
A cow walking backwards.

What did the snake say when it was offered a piece of cheese?
Thanks, I'll just have a slither.

What gets bigger the more you take away from it?
A hole.

I went to the optician's to collect my glasses and guess who I bumped into?
Everyone!

What's the difference between a nail and a boxer?
One gets knocked in and one gets knocked out.

Knock knock.
Who's there?
Scott.
Scott who?
Scott nothing to do with you.

Why did the Mexican throw his wife off the cliff?
Tequila!

What did the rabbit say to the carrot?
It was nice gnawing you.

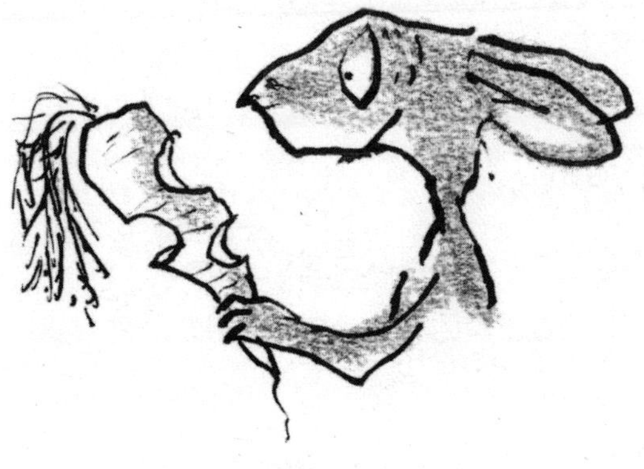

What do you get when you cross a chicken with a cement mixer?
A bricklayer.

Waiter, Waiter, I can't eat this soup. Call the manager.
It's no use, Madam. He won't eat it either.

Doctor, Doctor, I've broken my arm in two places.
Well, don't go there again.

My dog has no nose.
Really, how does he smell?
Terrible!

What kind of tree has hands?
A palm tree.

Why are hairdressers such good drivers?
They know all the short cuts.

What do you call a woman
with a sheep on her head?
Baa-baa-ra.

Why is a sofa like a roast turkey?
Because it's full of stuffing.

Why did the tuna go to Hollywood?
She wanted to be a starfish.

Why was the baby ant confused?
Because all his uncles were ants.

What has six legs but only uses four?
A man on a horse.

What's the tallest building?
A library because it has so many stories.

What do you call a pig with no clothes on?
Streaky bacon.

What happened when two fat men were in a race?
One ran in short bursts and the other ran in burst shorts.

Why did your brother wear a wet t-shirt all day?
The label said wash and wear.

What's white and yellow and travels at 160 mph?
A train driver's egg sandwich.

Why do some people like eating snails?
Because they don't like fast food.

PIANIST: Do you think I have a gift for playing?
DAD: No, but I'll give you a gift for stopping.

What do you call a man who forgets to put his pants on?
Nicholas.

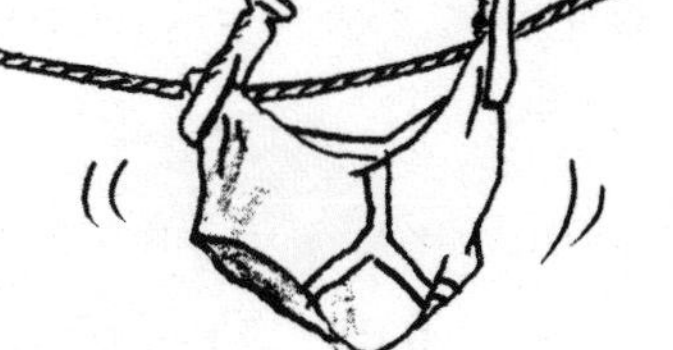

How do you know that carrots are good for your eyesight?
Have you ever seen a rabbit wearing glasses?

Did you hear about the man on a seafood diet?
If he saw food, he ate it.

Why is school like a shower?
One wrong turn and you're in hot water.

What begins with a P and ends with an E and has a million letters in it?
A Post Office.

What kind of crisps can fly?
Plane.

What do you call a sleeping dinosaur?
A dinosnore.

Knock knock.
Who's there?
Justin.
Justin who?
Justin in time for school, ha ha.

What happens to a cat if it eats a lemon?
It turns into a sourpuss.

Why did Horrid Henry take an empty doughnut to the dentist?
He wanted to get a filling.

Why is the letter T like an island?
Because it's in the middle of water.

Why does a seagull live near the sea?
If it lived near the bay, it'd be a bagel.

What song did they play when the baker got married?
Here crumbs the bride.

What do you call a boy with a spade on his head?
Doug.

What do you call a boy without a spade on his head?
Douglas.

How do you make an octopus laugh?
Ten tickles.

Which bird succeeds?
A budgie without any teeth.

What's a pelican's favourite dish?
Anything that fits the bill.

What did the little bird say to the big bird?
Peck on someone your own size.

What do you call a man who likes doing exercise?
Jim.

What's always coming, but never arrives?
Tomorrow.

How did the baker get an electric shock?
He stood on a bun and a current ran up his leg.

Who gets the sack as soon as he starts work?
A postman.

What goes, "Quick-quick!"?
A duck with the hiccups.

What do you call a clumsy bee?
A tumble bee.

Why did the girl throw the butter out of the window?
To see a butter fly.

Why couldn't the chicken find her eggs?
She mislaid them.

When's the best time to buy a bird?
When it's going "cheep cheep".

What happens if you call 666?
You get an upside-down policeman.

What do you call a man with a paper bag on his head?
Russell.

Why did Singing Soraya climb the ladder?
To reach the high notes.

Why did the boy climb the ladder?
He wanted to get to high school.

Why is your pet always smiling?
Because it's a grinny pig.

What do you call a man with a truck on his head?
Laurie.

What's worse than an elephant with a sore trunk?
A centipede with sore feet.

Why can't you tell
Humpty Dumpty
a joke?
Because he'll crack up.

What did one wall say to the other wall?
Meet you at the corner.

Waiter, Waiter, what do you call this?
It's bean soup, sir.
I don't care what it's been –
what is it now?

Why did the chicken cross the road?
To get to the shop.
Did you find that funny? Well, neither did the chicken because the shop was closed.

Why did the girl study on the aeroplane?
She wanted a higher education

Why couldn't the pirate play cards?
Because he was standing on the deck.

What do you call a piece of wood with nothing to do?
Bored.

Doctor, Doctor, I feel like a racehorse.
Take one of these every four laps.

Why did the banana go to the doctor?
He wasn't peeling well.

What do you call two robbers?
A pair of knickers.

What do you call an eight-legged cat?
An octopussy..

Why was the computer so cold?
Because its windows were open.

How did the bubblegum cross the road?
It was stuck to the chicken's foot.

What do you call a quiet bee?
A mumble bee.

EVEN MORE PURPLE JOKES

PETER: Henry, look, my tongue's gone purple.

HENRY: **Bleccch! Go and stick it out at Margaret.**

PETER: Will that help?

HENRY: **No, but I don't like Margaret.**

What's purple and leaps from a tree?

A squirrel.

Why is it purple?

Because it choked on a nut.

What colour do you get when you pull a burp?
Burp-pull.

What's purple and rides a horse?
Alexander the Grape.

MARGARET: Knock Knock.
SUSAN: Who's there?
MARGARET: The purple.
SUSAN: The purple who?
MARGARET: The purple who live next door.

What's purple with a hundred hairy legs?
I don't know, but there's one running up your leg.

What's a cat's favourite colour?
Purrrrrrr-ple.

What's big, purple and ugly?
You!

What do you call a purple dinosaur with a banana in each ear?
Anything you like -
he can't hear you.

HORRID HENRY: **What rhymes with red?**

LAZY LINDA: Bed.

HORRID HENRY: **What rhymes with green?**

PERFECT PETER: Bean

HORRID HENRY: **What rhymes with blue?**

RUDE RALPH: **Boo!**

HORRID HENRY: **What rhymes with purple?**

BEEFY BERT: I dunno.

Do you?

Horrid Henry would like to thank all the Purple Hand Gang members who sent in their totally brilliant, utterly wicked jokes.

Mia, Leicester
George, London
Jordan, Scarborough
Olivia, Rotherham
Cristina, Liverpool
Matt,Eastleigh
Nadine, UK
Murtaza, Sharjah
Izzy, Wigan

Raahul, Harrow
Katie, Liverpool
Mileena, Ipswich
Kapitalina, Antwerp
Caitlin, Dunedin
Ollie, Perthshire
David, Glasgow
Alex, Scunthorpe
Jodie, UK

Lily, UK
Gemma, Birmingham
Megan, South Woodham
Bilal Ahmed, Halifax
Abigail, England
Shyla, India
Kayaiya, London
Max, Gatley
Aminath, UK
Saaraj, Preston
Lauren, Hampshire
Jack, Doncaster
Phillipa, Coventry
Mitchell, London
Rebekah, Shropshire
Charlotte, Birmingham
Maisie, Rugby
Lois, Preston
Imogine, Manchester
Shauna, Nottingham
Jasmin, Leeds
Farwah, Luton
Rohail, London
Cameron, Lincolnshire
Alysha, England
Ari, UK
Ellie, UK
Rahul, England
Chantel, Norwich
Calum, Manchester
Emma, New Milton
Dana, Barwell
Kirsten, Greystone
Kelly, London
Beth, Lancaster
Messy, London
Maria, England
Chazii, Cambridge
Faye, Enfield
Alex, Slough
Sally, Trowbridge
Sahar, London
Bethany, England
Rico, London

Shane-Deon, London
Rebecca, Truro
Lauren, Leeds
Rachel, St Helens
Megan, Romford
Jasmine, Shropshire
Megan, Manchester
Eleanor, Chorley
Ryan, Kincardine
Ben, Wigan
Holly, UK
Benjamin, Leicester
Sannah, Birmingham
Liam, London
Libby, Coventry
David, Flintshir
Tiegan, UK
Evie, Epsom
Alfie, Essex
Kerry, Coventry
Robbie, Sedbergh
Ben, Milverton
Hannah, Blackburn

Bethany, Matlock
Suneet, Dublin
Kimran, Birmingham
Amana, London
Kayleigh, Ireland
Bethany, London
Leah, Bradford
Jennifer, Northampton
Courtney, Andover
Jessica, Warrington
Ben, London
Megan, Bury
Louise, Stoke on Trent
Britney, UK
Emma, Liverpool
Francesca, Dubai
Rebekah, UK
Kirsten, Glasgow
Aimee, Leeds
Holly, Blackburn
Ellie, Liverpool
Yasmine, Cowley

Ellie, Yorkshire
Miriam, Gloucester
Jasmine, Aylesbury
Bradley, UK
Lucy, Oldham
Talha, Manchester
Orla, England
Bobbi, Liverpool
Shea, Armagh
Leah, Manchester
Chloe, UK
Emma, England
Ellie, Wirral
Ellie, Littleborough
Danielle, Basingstoke
Mia, London
Lauren, Liverpool
Dominic, Ellesmere Port
Everette, Baltimore
Madeline, Leeds
Caitlin, Dublin
Roshni, London
Craig, Bishops Stortford
Lucia, London
Libby, Bolton
Cara, Norwich
Luca, Brighton & Hove
Joe, Derby
Mia, Manchester
Alisha, Mexico City
Kaisha, England
Joshua, Swindon
Sammy, UK
Susiksha, England
Ben, Hull
Lucy, UK
Jasmin, Wolverhampton
Sam, Bradford
Ahsan, London
Jay, South Ockendon
Lewis, London
Holly, Chatham
Jack, London
Morgan, Scotland
Mark, Leicester
Tammy, Sheffield

Jade, Hastings
Leah, London
Ben, Taunton
Rebecca, Harrogate
Callum, Tividale
Yusuf, London
James, Lisbon
Zoe, Birmingham
Sarah, Nottingham
Jacob, Liverpool
Ellis, Malvern
Samuel, Ajman
Lauren, Dollingstown
Teesta, Mumbai
Zoya, Manchester
Maryam, London
Saheem, Northampton
Caitlin, Durham
Caleb, Chongqing
Jess, Swanwick
Marie, Hampshire
Mairi, Stirling
Grace, London
Lewis, Newcastle
Chelsea-May, Redditch
Emma, Cumbernauld
Neil, Dundalk
Jake, Bristol
Bob, New York
Katie, St Albans
Evie, Manchester
Mary, London
Charlie, Woking
Eve, Monmouthshire
Mariam, Birmingham
Tony, Glasgow
Daniel, London
Rachel, Jakarta
Kanisha, Bangalore
Harry, Stone
Katie, Wanstead
Julia, Oswestry
Tyler, Wakefield
Lilly, Paris
Hannah, Ipswich

Irandip, Wolverhampton
Henna, Oldham
Thomas, UK
Amal, Birmingham
Lillee, Plymouth
Haroon, Birmingham
Hassan, Dublin
Lucas, Guernsey
Ned, Purley
Teeba, London
Mhairi, Torphins
Paige, Newark
Erin, Barrhead
Lucia, Margate
Toby, Congleton
Alessio, London
Mia, Kent
Alice, Swadlincote
Anant, Mumbai
Kamilla, Stourport
Harrison, Manchester
Christopher, UK
Alex, Essex
Rebecca, Middlesbrough
Joel, Peterhead
Kirsty, Belfast
Elizabeth, London
Jasmine, Portsmouth
Lydia, Cleveland
Alice, England
Shannon, Tadworth
Nikita, Torrington
Joshua, Essex
Ashleigh, Oldham
Isabel, Exeter
Adam, Douglas
Pearse, Dublin
Jessica, Liverpool
Presley, Manchester
Brandon, Crewe
Dylan, Shrewsbury
Lucy, Chatham
Ellie, Mistley
Charlotte, Farnham
Jake, Dublin
Shania, Solihull

Nathan, Preston
Rihanna, London
Sabbir, London
Shreyas, Milton Keynes
Emily, Dublin
Rhianna, Oxford
Jane, London
Emily, London
Joey, London
James, Leeds
Talia, Oldham
Alisha, Birmingham
Darcy, Durham
Hafsa, Manchester
Bláthnaid, Carrickmore
Vikram, Newcastle
Nina, UK
Megan, London
Hashim, London
Charlie, Bristol
Adam, London
Britney, Newcastle
Finn, Middlesbrough
Patrick, Belfast
Catherine, Liverpool
Louise, Pontypridd
Salom, Luton
Jake, Manchester
Kelsey, Retford
Niamh, Highwycombe
Gabriella, Durban
Lily, Cape Town
Georgia, Hull
Charlotte, London
Zaynab, Birmingham
Colm, Kerry
Antara, Kolkata
Thea, Chichester
Matthew, Walsall
Faith, Kent
Linards, Ireland
Liberty, Haringey
Kiera, Leamington
Aidan, Manchester
Ben, Sutton

Susanna, London
Conor, Dunbar
Luke, Cork
Ewan, UK
Sana, Al Ain
Georgia, Reigate
Louie, Reading
Sara, London
Clio, Newtown
Michelle, London
Abinaya, Stevenage
Josie, London
Lauren, UK
Callum, Paisley
Eli, Wales
Nicole, Dundrod
Teuta, Harrow
Jessica, Bedford
Afiq, Singapore
Tamsin, Thanet
Bobbie, Grimsby
Megan, Wolverhampton
Sharna, Westcliff
Tyler, Paddock Wood
Jodie, Shropshire
Shah, London
Gemma, Johannesburg
Brittany, Victoria
Shaye, London
Maya, Tipton
Sian, Plymouth
Holly, Lancaster
Dhruv, Chennai
Rosie, Coventry
Toby, Derby
Camila, London
Jessica, Eastbourne
Chloe, Kirkby
Liam, Carlisle
Jed, Newcastle
Esha, Rochdale
Alfie, Coventry
Yasmin, Manchester
Isabelle, Scotland
Jessica, Nottingham

Sophie, Saltash
Jolene, Belfast
Kyra, UK
Jack, Dagenham
Mohammed, Qatar
Hannah, Dunfermline
Aishwarya, Lusaka
Oliver, Croydon
Saz, New York
Anzum, London
Abi, Newcastle
GuanMin, Singapore
Jackie, London
Cassy, Liverpool
Zara, Birmingham
Katie, Oswestry
Samuel, Andover
Stephanie, Newbury
Olivia, UK
Gemma, Luton
Kieran, UK
Jada, London
Phil, Liverpool

Maxine, Surrey
Paul, Liverpool
Eleanor, Benfleet
Luke, Oldham
Nerissa, Eastbourne
Mayyah, Northampton
Tegan, UK
Evie, Leicestershire
Emily, Leipzig
Jude, Richmond
Harrison, Brereton
Monet, London
Sian, Tamworth
Adrienne, Northampton
Hannah, Newport
Sajeevan, London
Grace, West Midlands
Ella, Waltham Cross
Jaya, Orpington
Gemma, UK
Jade, Lydd
Liberty, Portsmouth
Megan, Wales

Emily, Bridgend
Moo, USA
Donna, England
Clio, Powys
Jasmine, Rugby
Michael, Lochgilphead
Alexia, Wimbledon
Leela, Broadstairs
Thomas, Tapei City
Rory, Shipley
Chloe, England
Samantha, Caterham
Kirstin, Watford
Shazna, Woking
Amy, Shrewsbury
Ceri, Forfar
Leilla, Surbiton
Owen, Harwich
Sophie, Nottinghamshire
Evie, Grimsby
Olivia, Plymouth
Jaya, West Yorkshire
Adil, Preston
Caitlin, Kilsyth
Nicole, Billericay
Lauren, England
Liberty, Nottingham
Chantelle, York
Shanaj, London
Anya, Northampton
Max, London
Oliver, Sidcup
Maebh, Co. Cork
Libby, Manchester
Jodi, Glasgow
Millie, Guernsey
Joshua, Walsall
Morgan, Glasgow
Jadene, Helston
William, Tunbridge Wells
Deana, Newark
Chloe, Nottingham
Luke, Derby
Benjamin, Studham
Jake, Leeds
Stephen, Rushall

Millie, Rugby
Marie, Rushall
Josh, Basildon
Lia, Blackpool
Jonathan, Ipswich
Zac, Brighton
Celie, London
Georgia, England
Ivan, East Kilbride
Jaz, Kent
Kelsey, London
Claudia, Cirencester
Reilly, Derbyshire
Kirandeep, Coventry
Elysia, UK
Liam, Norwich
Aaqib, Bradford
Ellie, Darlington
Katie, Roscommon
Lily, Rushden
Sandhya, England
Kishan, London
Lauren, Dunstable
Lauren, Southend on Sea
Gemma, Falkirk
Courtney, Sunderland
Priya, Birmingham
Connor, Burntisland
Georgia, Marton
Yagoda, London
Tracey, Airdrie
Isaac, Nottingham
Megan, Whitely
Nasar, Burton
Tom, London
Abigail, Peterborough
Amber, Hartlepool
Annabelle, Wilmslow
Elliot, Taunton
Charley, Nottingham
Raeece, Manchester
Zain, Manchester
Keita, Preston
Georgia, Blackpool
Cariad, Essex
Zhanae, Nottingham

Myles, Manchester
Devon, Egham
Elana, Scotland
Mollie, Manchester
Ethan, Nottingham
Musab, Manchester
Ella, Swansea
Maryam, Didcot
Callum, Kirkcudbright
Kitty, Coventry
Rebecca, London
Finley, Lee on the Solent
India, Clevedon
Joe, Stoke
Bobbie-May, Kingstanding
Sam, Belfast
Ella, Leicestershire
Emily, Hockley
Toni, Lincoln
Susie, London
Krishma, Staffs
Farhan, London

Louise, Great Wyrley
Madina, England
Manoli, London
Melvin, London
Marsha, Ascot
Fenton, Hoghton
Georgia, London
Courtney, Liverpool
Clara, Chichester
Megan, Spalding
Leanne, Glasgow
Richard, Longford
Georgia, Sheffield
Ali, Harlow
Zachary, Nantwich
Jake, Wolverhampton
Morgan, Barnsley
Jack, UK
Evie, Willenhall
Ryan Manchester

HORRID HENRY BOOKS

Horrid Henry

Horrid Henry and the Secret Club

Horrid Henry Tricks the Tooth Fairy

Horrid Henry's Nits

Horrid Henry Gets Rich Quick
(previously *Horrid Henry Strikes it Rich)*

Horrid Henry's Haunted House

Horrid Henry and the Mummy's Curse

Horrid Henry's Revenge

Horrid Henry and the Bogey Babysitter

Horrid Henry's Stinkbomb

Horrid Henry's Underpants

Horrid Henry meets the Queen

Horrid Henry and the Mega-Mean Time Machine

Horrid Henry and the Football Fiend

Horrid Henry's Christmas Cracker

Horrid Henry and the Abominable Snowman

Horrid Henry Robs the Bank

Horrid Henry Wakes the Dead

Horrid Henry Rocks

Horrid Henry and the Zombie Vampire

Horrid Henry's Monster Movie

Horrid Henry's Nightmare

Horrid Factbooks

Horrid Henry's Bodies
Horrid Henry's Bugs
Horrid Henry's Dinosaurs
Horrid Henry's Food
Horrid Henry's Kings and Queens
Horrid Henry's Sports

Joke Books

Horrid Henry's Joke Book
Horrid Henry's Jolly Joke Book
Horrid Henry's Mighty Joke Book
Horrid Henry's Hilariously Horrid Joke Book
Horrid Henry's Purple Hand Gang Joke Book
Horrid Henry's All Time Favourite Joke Book

Colour books

Horrid Henry's Big Bad Book
Horrid Henry's Wicked Ways
Horrid Henry's Evil Enemies
Horrid Henry Rules the World
Horrid Henry's House of Horrors
Horrid Henry's Dreadful Deeds
Horrid Henry Shows Who's Boss

Horrid Henry's Fearsome Four

Horrid Henry's A-Z of Everything Horrid